EDINBURGH
City Beautiful

John McDermott has been taking photographs for over 15 years and has a well-established company called www.YouKeepEveryPhoto.com.

John is also a talented writer and composer. His first novel, *Seb*, about a 21-year-old Glaswegian, will be published in Spring 2008. He will be taking his new rock opera *Jesus Christ Risen Star* to the Edinburgh Fringe in 2008. His debut single *Follow* with his band the Jay Jays was released in November 2007. He played all the instruments and provided the vocals.

He is a double graduate from the University of Glasgow with a Bachelor of Science (honours) in Biochemistry and a Bachelor of Divinity with distinction, followed by two years' research in theology.

John loves taking photographs, especially at weddings, directing his subjects to participate in his works of art.

His other sites include:

- www.iLoveEdinburgh.com
- www.EdinburghCityBeautiful.com
- www.KiltedPhotographer.com
- www.JohnMcDermott.co.uk

EDINBURGH
City Beautiful

John McDermott

breedon **books**
PUBLISHING

First published in Great Britain in 2008 by The Breedon Books Publishing
Company Limited, Breedon House, 3 The Parker Centre, Derby, DE21 4SZ.

**To all my family, especially my Mum,
thanks again for all your help.**

ISBN 978-1-85983-626-2
Printed and bound in China.

Contents

Foreword

Edinburgh is the capital of Scotland and is one of the most interesting and spectacular cities in Europe, perhaps the world. There is so much to do and see, with every corner and turn offering a photo opportunity. Edinburgh Castle is a must to see and the Royal Mile has to be enjoyed at a leisurely pace so that you do not miss anything. The New Town is completely different from the Old Town, but both add to the unique charm of the city. There are many ways to spend your money, either shopping in one of the many malls or buying a round of drinks in Rose Street. If it is culture you are after then Edinburgh offers many museums, especially the National Galleries of Scotland or the People's Museum. If you want fresh air then there are plenty of walks and hills to climb. Leith offers a change from the tourist trail and Dean Village takes you back in time to when life was less hectic. Edinburgh is indeed a city beautiful.

When I started photographing Edinburgh for this book I was overwhelmed: so many places, so much history, what if I missed something out? Then, as I was photographing the Grassmarket, I saw the Glasgow coat of arms above a pub. I knew then that although Edinburgh was not 'my city' as Glasgow was, I still belonged. As I took my photograph I turned around and saw a tourist taking the same photograph. I explained that I was from Glasgow, and while talking to her I realised how similar the cities are. I enjoyed my seven days photographing Edinburgh in October 2007, and I am so proud to have captured it as I have. I am sure that this book will inspire the reader to open their eyes and see all that Edinburgh has to offer.

Introduction

The Old Town of Edinburgh has been at the heart of Scottish history for centuries. There was a fort on the Castle Rock in Iron Age times and by the 12th century Edinburgh had become a town and royal burgh. After David I founded the Abbey of the Holy Rude in the royal park, Edinburgh developed down the long road between the castle and Holyrood.

By the 16th century James IV had created the beginnings of a royal palace at Holyrood and had made Edinburgh known throughout Europe. By the time James V's daughter, Mary, Queen of Scots, was born in 1542 the pattern of the Old Town with its high 'lands' (many-storeyed tenements), narrow wynds and closes was well established. By this time too the town had been enclosed by walls. The King's Wall was built c.1450–75; the Flodden Wall in 1514–60 and the Telfer Wall in 1628–36, which stretched down to the Grassmarket and south just beyond Greyfriars.

The main thoroughfare, the Royal Mile, consisted of several streets: Castlehill, the Lawnmarket, and the High Street down to the Netherbow Port. The Canongate was actually outside the city walls and was a burgh in its own right until 1856. It had more of a country atmosphere too.

In the tightly-packed lands higher up the Royal Mile all levels of society met. Judges and dukes rubbed shoulders with merchants and commons. The Old Town was the home of the Scottish Parliament, until the Union with the English of 1707, as well as the law courts, learning and commerce. All classes lived and worked there together. Following its 16th-century suspension the Scottish Parliament reconvened in the Old Town in 1999, at the Mound, close to its earlier home. A permanent Parliament building has been built at the other end of the Old Town in Holyrood.

After 1767 the development of the New Town led to 'the Great Flitting' across the valley Mound to its classical elegance. The Old Town was left with the ghosts of the past and an ever-increasing population of the poor. Disease and decay endured where once the men of learning and genius had stood.

Today life is being breathed back into the Old Town. It has been declared a conservation area; the Old Town Renewal Trust has been formed to care for it and old buildings are being restored. People are returning to live and work at the heart of one of Europe's most historic cities.

In 1995 the Old Town of Edinburgh was declared a World Heritage Site.

Pre-History

Pictured right, **dolerite**, an igneous rock from Caldercruix, near Edinburgh, that cooled from molten magma around 300 million years ago, is built into the new Scottish Parliament buildings. This fact is written in the pavement on the road outside the building (pictured below).

Dynamic Earth tells the story of our planet, the 'Mother Earth of all adventure experiences'. It is a great family day out. Exhibits include the Future Dome, the Time Machine, the Tropical Rainforest and Polar Extremes.

Opposite: Outside the museum are fossils from the Jurassic Sea that are over 150 million years old.

Jurassic Sea
150 million years ago

Flying Reptile (top)
Pterodactylus antiquus

Ammonite (bottom)
Psiloceras johnstoni

Arthur's Seat, Salisbury Crags and the Pentland Hills

Arthur's Seat is the main peak of the group of hills which form most of Holyrood Park, a remarkably wild piece of highland landscape in the centre of the city of Edinburgh, about a mile to the east of Edinburgh Castle. The hill rises above the city to a height of 251m (823ft), providing excellent panoramic views of the city and is a popular walk.

The Salisbury Crags are a series of 150ft cliffs at the top of a subsidiary spur of Arthur's Seat. They can be seen from outside the new Scottish Parliament buildings.

The Pentland Hills occupy a special place in the Scottish psyche. Forming the backdrop to the nation's capital, their geography has shaped the success of the Lothians. They have played a role in the drama of Scottish history and our poets and authors have written about them with iconic status.

Recent History

Now we move into the 16th century.

It is possible to view a section of the **Flodden Wall**, the old city wall built in the wake of Scotland's defeat at Flodden in 1513, in which King James IV was killed, beside Greyfriar's Kirk.

Flodden was the worst defeat in Scottish history. However, the wall was never needed. Evidence of the old city wall can also be seen on the corner of **Teviot Place** and **Bristo Place**, with the date 1513 included in the brickwork. Edinburgh is proud of its history and there are many commemorative plaques located around the city. It has always been a God-fearing city and was at the heart of the Scottish Reformation.

Above the main door of the **Writer's Museum** on the Royal Mile, carved in stone, are the words 'Feare the Lord, and depart from evil.'

This plaque on the wall is in both English and Greek. It quotes from the Gospel of John, chapter five, verse nine and encourages the reader to 'Search the Scriptures.'

This plaque tells the passer-by to 'Love God above all and your neighbour as yourself.' This was entirely appropriate when families were living cheek by jowl in tenements housing up to 20 families.

The **Glasgow coat of arms** can be seen above these shops in the Grassmarket, beside the Edinburgh coat of arms. Even though the two cities are separated by almost 50 miles, they consider themselves to be neighbours.

GIFTS ~ CRAFTS ~ TOYS

This beautiful plaque is of the **Clan Johnston crest**, the clan who fought against the English armies at the Battle of Solway in 1378. Their motto is *Nunquam non paratus,* which translates as 'never unprepared'.

The old banks are reflected in the windows of modern banks. Even today they are promising you the best value for money.

There is a good mixture of commuters, residents and tourists in Edinburgh, and it has been an important city both historically and financially. This clock shows office workers just how long they have left on their breaks, so there is no excuse for being late.

The **One O'Clock Gun** in Edinburgh Castle famously goes off at the same time every afternoon.

This plaque on the wall, dating from 1735, quotes Job, chapter seven, verse six: 'My days are swifter than a weaver's shuttle.'

The large archways of the **North Bridge** join the Old and New Towns, near to the south entrance of Waverley train station. The Old Town is compared to Hyde while the New Town is Jekyll as they are so vastly different.

Coates Crescent is not one of the most famous Edinburgh tourist sites, but it is a great find in the New Town.

Edinburgh residents love their small balconies outside the windows. Some balconies even have their own trees as residents have to improvise because many do not have their own front gardens.

Some crescents are extremely uniform in design; apart from the numbers outside, you might forget which house you live in.

Other houses are more grand than those around them, so it would be impossible to keep up with the Joneses here.

Further building works and improvements are taking place in the Old Town. This building, on the Royal Mile near the castle, won the award for reconstruction in 1971 .

There are many ghost stories and ghost tours around the city. There is one famous story of a bagpiper who piped in a tunnel under the Royal Mile from the castle to Holyrood, but he mysteriously vanished. Perhaps this bagpiper is his ghost!

No matter where you are in Edinburgh, you can always hear the sound of bagpipes. They are everywhere!

Famous People and Dogs

Edinburgh has had its fair share of celebrities, but the most well known is a wee dog. **Greyfriar's Bobby** was a faithful Skye terrier who watched over the grave of his master John Gray, who was a market constable in the Grassmarket. He watched the grave for over 14 years before he died in 1872. He was given a special collar by the Lord Provost so he would not be mistaken for a stray. This statue was erected with permission of the Baroness Burdett Coutts.

Every day at one o'clock, as the gun fired, Greyfriar's Bobby went to this pub to be fed.

The faithful dog is buried in front of the church.

Opposite: There is no mystery about who this statue portrays, with his trademark deerstalker. **Sherlock Holmes** stands looking at the traffic at Picardy Place. The statue is in memory of his creator, **Sir Arthur Conan Doyle,** and was unveiled on 24 June 1991 by Professor G.D. Chisholm, president of the Royal College of Surgeons in Edinburgh.

Sir Arthur Conan Doyle was born at **No. 11 Picardy Place** on 22 May 1859. Picardy Place was named after a 17th-century settlement of French weavers.

Many famous people of the past also have their names on plaques outside their old houses. **James Clerk Maxwell**, Natural Philosopher, was born here at 14 India Street on 13 June 1831. He was the formulator of the electromagnetic theory of light and pioneer of statistical mathematics. His house is now home to the International Centre for Mathematical Studies.

The Earl of Moray lived at **No. 28 Moray Place**, one of the finest houses in the Moray estates, designed by James Gillespie Graham.

There is a plaque in Edinburgh Castle to commemorate **Thomas Randolph, Earl of Moray**, who was a distinguished soldier and diplomat who recovered the castle in 1313 after it had been in the hands of the English.

A plaque states that **Henry Broughman** was born in this house on 19 September 1778.

Sir James Young Simpson lived in this house from 1845 to 1870, and in 1847 he discovered the anaesthetic power of chloroform. He is buried in St Cuthbert's graveyard, pictured below.

The house of **Robert Louis Stevenson** at 17 Heriot Row. Robert Louis (Balfour) Stevenson (13 November 1850–3 December 1894) was a Scottish novelist, poet and travel writer, and a leading representative of Neo-romanticism in English literature. His most well-read novels are *Treasure Island* (1883) and *The Strange Case of Dr Jekyll and Mr Hyde* (1886). His other novels include *Kidnapped* (1886), the *Master of Ballantrae* (1889) and *New Arabian Nights* (1882).

Outside Stevenson's house, on a lamp post, there is a quote from his poem *Leerie*:

*But I, when I am stronger and
  can choose what I'm to do,
O Leerie, I'll go round at night
  and light the lamps with you!
For we are very lucky, with a
  lamp before the door,
And Leerie stops to light it as he
  lights so many more;
And O! Before you hurry by
  with ladder and with light,
O Leerie, see a little child and
  nod to him tonight!*

Stevenson would perhaps have watched this felled tree grow.

He may have had a key to enter the private gardens.

William Graham LLD, educationalist, lived here between 1850 and 1871. He was the pioneer of secondary education for girls and the principal founder of the Scottish institution for the education of young ladies, between 1834 and 1870.

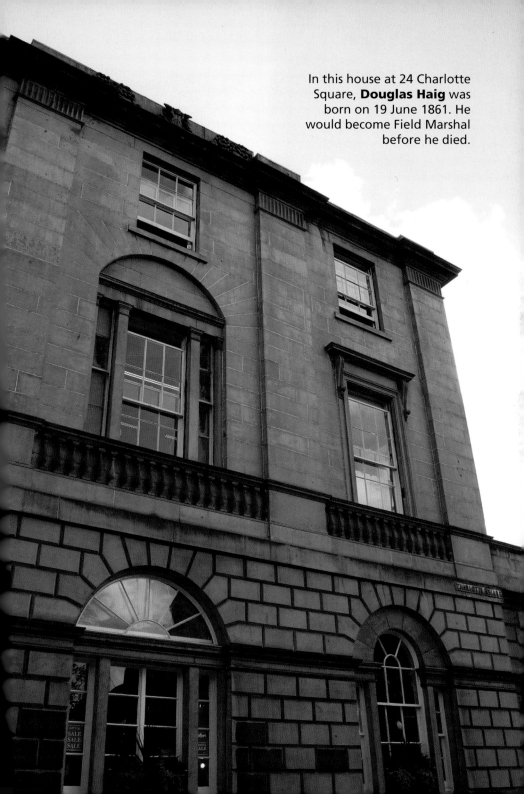

In this house at 24 Charlotte Square, **Douglas Haig** was born on 19 June 1861. He would become Field Marshal before he died.

Alexander Graham Bell, the inventor of the telephone, was born at No. 16 South Charlotte Street on 3 March 1847.

William Dick (1793–1866) was born within this close on 6 May 1793. He was the founder of the Edinburgh Veterinary College, incorporated in the University of Edinburgh in 1951 as the Royal (Dick) School of Veterinary Studies and instituted as the Faculty of Veterinary Medicine in 1964.

The houses (left and opposite) originally dated from 1623 but were rebuilt in 1962.

Edinburgh Castle

The rock on which Edinburgh Castle stands was formed 70 million years ago. Recent archaeological excavations in Edinburgh Castle have uncovered evidence that Bronze-Age man was living on the rock as long ago as 850BC. Two thousand years ago, during the Iron Age, the rock had a hill fort settlement on its summit. Edinburgh Castle is an ancient fortress which, from its position atop Castle Rock, dominates the skyline of the city of Edinburgh. It is Scotland's second most-visited tourist attraction after the Kelvingrove Art Gallery and Museum in Glasgow. As it stands today though, few of the castle's structures pre-date the 16th century, with the notable exception of St Margaret's Chapel, the oldest surviving building in

Edinburgh, which dates from the early 12th century. The castle has a strong connection with the army. Sentries still stand watch at the castle gatehouse between 6pm and 9am, with responsibility for guarding the Honours of Scotland, the Crown Jewels and the Stone of Destiny. Against the spectacular backdrop of Edinburgh Castle on the Esplanade, the world-famous Massed Pipes and Drums, together with the Massed Military Bands of the Band of the Royal Regiment of Scotland, were among those who took part in the Military Tattoo in August 2007.

Signs of the Tattoo after it had finished.

The castle is a five-star tourist attraction.

There is lots of room for all the pipe bands and performers to move about during the Tattoo.

Many thousands queue up to see the spectacular event.

Before entering the castle there are many memorials on the Esplanade.

46

A **Statue of Earl Haig**, who was born in Charlotte Square.

This statue is of **Field Marshal his Royal Highness, Frederick Duke of York and Albany, KG** Commander in Chief of the British Royal Army.

This is the tomb of **Ensign Ewart of the Royal North British Dragoons**. At Waterloo, as sergeant, he captured the standard of the French 45th regiment, from which the eagle badge now worn by the Royal Scots Greys is derived. This tomb was erected to his memory in April 1938 by the officers, warrant officers, non-commissioned officers and men past and present of the Royal Scots Greys.

This soldier from the **Royal Scots Greys** stands guard on his horse in front of the castle. It was erected in memory of all those who gave their lives for their country in the Boer War of 1899–1902.

There is an eagle on the side above the word Waterloo.

This statue is in memory of the officers, non-commissioned officers and men of the **72nd Duke of Albany's Own Highlanders** who were killed in action or died from their wounds or disease during the campaign in Afghanistan in 1878–79.

48

This Celtic cross is in memory of **Kenneth Douglas Mackenzie**, who served for 42 years in the 92nd Highlanders.

The Celtic cross above, is for those **men and horses** who died in the South African wars.

This monument remembers those who died in the **suppression of the native army of India**.

Opposite: **the main entrance** to the castle would have been a frightening or welcoming sight depending on whose side you were on.

Near this spot in 1625 Sir William Alexander of Menstrie, Earl of Stirling, received sasine or lawful possession of the royal province of Nova Scotia by the symbolic ceremony of delivery of earth and stone from Castlehill by a representative of the king. Also here (1625–37) the Scottish Baronets of Nova Scotia received sasine of their distant baronies. The plaque was presented by the province of Nova Scotia.

This is where guards stand for hours on end without coffee breaks.

The memorial to **William Wallace** at the front entrance was erected by the Corporation of Edinburgh under Captain Hugh Reid's bequest, and was unveiled on 28 May 1929.

The memorial to **Robert the Bruce** was also erected by the Corporation of Edinburgh under Captain Hugh Reid's bequest and unveiled on the same day, 28 May 1929.

The gatehouse was built in 1887 as an impressive show front to replace the plain 17th-century outer gate. Inside was accommodation for the main guard, detention cells and a court-martial room.

The old guardhouse was built in 1853 as the main guardhouse with the detention cells added in 1866. After being replaced by the present gatehouse it was used as the quartermaster's stores.

The 17th-century **inner barrier** was an intermediate defensive barrier with its own ditch and drawbridge. It was built on the site of the 16th-century inner gate.

This plaque is in memory of **Sir William Kirkcaldy of Grange**, who was justly reputed to be the one of the best soldiers and most accomplished cavaliers of his time.

The Portcullis Gate (1574–77) was built after the Long Siege of 1571–73, replacing the damaged mediaeval Constable's Tower. The top storey, the Argyle Tower, was added in 1887.

The long stairs and the main access to the summit are of the Castle Rock. The more gradual ascent of the present road was created in the 15th century to improve the passage of heavy guns into the castle.

The Argyle Battery (1730–32) was part of the improvements to the defences ordered by General Wade, famous for his military roads and bridges in the Highlands. Archaeologists are excavating part of the Argyle Battery to find out more about how the castle was defended.

These guns are 18-pounders, made in 1810.

There are great views over the city and Calton Hill towards the Firth of Forth.

The cart shed of 1746 was built in the aftermath of the 1745 Jacobite rising. It was built to hold 50 provisions carts supplying the large garrison of redcoats in the castle.

You can never get lost in the castle as there are plenty of signs.

The Governor's House (1742) was built as the official residence of the castle governor, with houses in the wings for the master gunner and the storekeeper.

Looking through one of the walls towards the Governor's House.

The New Barracks (1796–99) was the largest structure in the castle, built to accommodate a battalion of 600 men with their officers.

The Regimental Museum, through paintings, artefacts, silver and medals, tells their fascinating story, from formation to the present day. It is a story that mirrors the fortunes of the country. Whether in Europe, Asia, the Middle East, Africa or the Americas, members of the Regiment have followed the flag in the service of their country.

Foog's Gate was the main entrance to the citadel by the 17th century. The perimeter wall, looped for both cannon and musketry, was built in King Charles II's reign (1669–85).

Saint Margaret's Chapel.

Saint Margaret's Chapel is the oldest building in the castle and was built by King David I (1124–53) and dedicated to his mother, who died here in 1093. It was called then a fort on the 'hill of Agnes'. She was created a saint in 1250.

Mon's Meg is a giant mediaeval siege gun (508mm), presented to King James II in 1457 and used during wars against the English.

The dog cemetery is a small garden which was used during Queen Victoria's reign (1837–1901) as a burial place for regimental mascots and officer's dogs.

Mon's Meg once fired a large gunstone almost two miles.

Looking up inside the gun.

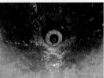

Taking aim, but not firing.

The Scottish National War Memorial (1927) was built in remembrance of those from Scotland who died in World War One. It is now a shrine to the memory of the fallen of the two world wars and of campaigns since 1945. Work is currently being carried out on it.

The Firewall Battery was rebuilt by King James V in 1540 on the line of the mediaeval defences.

The Half Moon Battery (1573–88) was a mighty artillery fortification built after the Long Siege of 1571–73 to protect the Royal Palace from bombardment. David's Tower, the residence of Robert the Bruce's son, King David II (1329–71), lies buried beneath the platform.

For 500 years, until the 19th century, the **Fore Well** was the castle's main water supply. It is 30 feet deep, but the water level was never enough to meet the demand.

The Royal Palace was the residence of the Stewart kings and queens in the 15th and 16th centuries. It was also the birthplace of King James VI in 1566 and the home of the Scottish Crown jewels, the Honours and the Stone of Destiny, returned to Scotland from Westminster Abbey in 1996.

The Great Hall (1503–13) was built for King James IV (1488–1513) as a majestic setting for ceremonial occasions. In 1650 it was converted into soldiers' barracks by Oliver Cromwell.

The Queen Anne building (c.1710) was built after the 1708 Jacobite rising as barracks for officers and the castle's gunners. It was also the first home of Mon's Meg in the castle.

If you listen carefully in **the dungeons** you can hear loud screams.

70

The side of the steep walls, which would have been impossible to climb.

Guards could watch for miles for any intruders and sound the alarm in plenty of time.

Watching the sunset beside the castle is breathtaking. You can see the castle and the church spires of the east of Edinburgh cutting through the red and orange sky.

The back of the castle photographed from beside the **Saltire Court** (below). The reflection of the castle can be seen in one of the court building windows.

Opposite: both old and new buildings in the Old Town with the castle in the background.

Old Town

The Old Town of Edinburgh, the capital of Scotland, is a UNESCO World Heritage Site. It has preserved its mediaeval plan and many Reformation-era buildings. One end is closed by the castle and the main artery, the Royal Mile (actually made up of four distinct streets, named Castlehill, the Lawnmarket, the High Street and the Canongate), leads away from it, down to the now-ruined Holyrood Abbey. Narrow closes (alleyways), often no more than a few feet wide, lead downhill on either side of the main spine in a herringbone pattern. Large squares mark the location of markets or surround major public buildings such as St Giles' Cathedral and the supreme courts. Other notable places include the Scottish Parliament building, the Palace of Holyroodhouse, the General Assembly Hall of the Church of Scotland, the Royal Museum of Scotland, Surgeons' Hall, the University of Edinburgh and numerous underground streets and vaults, relics of previous phases of construction. The street layout, typical of the old quarters of many northern European cities, is made especially picturesque in Edinburgh, where the castle perches on top of a rocky crag, the remnants of an extinct volcano, and the main street runs down the crest of a ridge from it.

You can not escape the cobbles anywhere in the Old Town, even here at St Giles' Cathedral.

Most of the back streets in Edinburgh are still cobblestones, which keeps the speed of the cars to a minimum.

Greyfriar's Kirk dates from Christmas Day 1620 and was the first church to be built in Edinburgh after the Reformation. It was built on the site of a Franciscan Friary dating from 1447–1560.

The National Covenant was signed in 1638 in the **Kirkyard**. The document was concerned about preserving the Reformation settlement free from Crown 'innovations'. The Kirkyard was established in 1562 and is believed to be haunted by the MacKenzie poltergeist from as far back as 1824. Many famous people are buried in the graveyard, including Robert and John Smith. Parts of the Flodden Wall can be seen in the Kirkyard, which is next to George Heriot's College.

The **Cowgate** is hidden underneath the bridges which join the Old and New Towns.

Old St Paul's Church is located at The Cowgate. It was founded in 1689, and it was an 18th-century refuge for Jacobites, a 19th-century Anglo-Catholic revival and a 20th-century centre of spirituality and service.

The North Bridge crosses over the Old Town and it is possible to look below on to the narrow streets. It was first built in 1763 and widened in 1876. The North Bridge was completely rebuilt in 1896–97 to span Waverley train station and raised 18 inches. The foundation stone was laid on 23 May 1896 and the bridge was opened on 15 September 1897 by the Right Hon. Sir Andrew McDonald, Lord Provost. The floodlighting was switched on by Councillor Eric Milligan, convenor of Lothian Region Council, on 22 November 1990 as part of the North Bridge refurbishment.

In the middle of the bridge there is a war memorial sculpted by Birnie Rhind (1853–1933), who was born in Edinburgh. He is best known for the Royal Scots Greys memorial (1905), the Black Watch (1908) and the King's Own Scottish Borderers (1919). The memorial remembers commissioned officers and men who died while fighting in the wars of the late 19th century.

The South Bridge was built almost 20 years after the North Bridge in 1787.

Above the shops on the North Bridge there is an old sign that states '**Protestant Institute of Scotland**.' Now the building is home to offices and an Italian restaurant.

Standing in the middle of the North Bridge, the **Scotsman** building and the **Carlton Hotel** can be seen.

The first edition of the *Scotsman* was published on 25 January 1817. The *Scotsman* then incorporated the smaller *Caledonian Mercury* in 1832.

The Carlton Hotel is located on the corner of the North Bridge and the Royal Mile. If you need to know anything then ask Angus, the chief concierge.

The **Bank of Scotland** was established in 1695, just off the Royal Mile. It employed its first female worker in 1916, 200 years later.

The motto above the front door, *'Tanto Uberior'* means 'So much more plentiful.'

Each room of the **Bank Hotel** on South Bridge is uniquely decorated to celebrate the life of a famous Scot, including Robert Burns and James Watt.

A plaque here states that 'This is the first building erected under the Improvement Act of 1867, the Right Honourable William Chambers of Glenormiston, Lord Provost.' By the middle of the 19th century, Edinburgh's Old Town had degenerated into little more than a slum. There were two main reasons for this. The first was the degeneration of the buildings and the second was the influx of working-class people to the city. With the concentration of building programmes on the New Town area of Edinburgh, no major private or public building projects had taken place in the Old Town for many decades and the buildings fell into a terrible state.

Tron Kirk was founded in 1636 by James Mylne. The Tron was a public weighing beam and if traders were selling short measures then they were hung from the beam by their ears. Members from St Giles first worshipped here. Some of the church was demolished to make way for the North and South bridges and, unfortunately, a great fire in 1824 destroyed most of the spire. It is no longer used as a place of worship but is home to the Old Town tourist information centre.

Magdalen Chapel was founded in 1547 by Janet Rynd as a chapel and hospice for several pensioners. It is not a grand chapel, but is home to the only pre-Reformation Scottish stained glass *in situ*. The spire dates from 1620. It was built to serve both as a religious chapel and also as a guildhall for the Incorporation of Hammermen and was planned by Mitchell MacQuhane then built by his wife Janet Rynd after his death. The Incorporation of Hammermen, a trade guild which consisted of all workers in metal, were the principal patrons of the chapel and the small hospital which adjoined the chapel, built in 1547.

Among its historical features are the four stained-glass roundels, the only pre-Reformation stained glass in Scotland still intact. The panelled arcading, recording gifts to the chapel and hospital, dating from 1585, is also of great interest. During and immediately following the Reformation in Scotland in the 15th century, the chapel was used for meetings of the Reformed Church in Scotland.

The National Library of Scotland was founded in 1682 and is one of the largest public libraries in the UK. The library is an information treasure trove of Scotland's history and culture, with millions of books, manuscripts and maps covering every subject.

There are some incredible carvings on the wall, including the one below, which is the Royal Coat of Arms of the United Kingdom, as used in Scotland. The Latin translates as 'No one provokes me with impunity.'

The National Museum of Scotland covers life, the universe and everything in it. Some of the exhibits are millions of years old; others are less than a decade old.

The City Art Centre is located at 2 Market Square. It has five floors of municipal art space and is mostly community based. It used to be an old warehouse before being converted.

The Fruitmarket Gallery is across the road from the City Arts Centre.

Fleshmarket Close originally descended from the Royal Mile to the meat market. Ian Rankin named one of his Rebus novels after this close.

As with all the closes, the stairs are very steep and can be dangerous in bad weather.

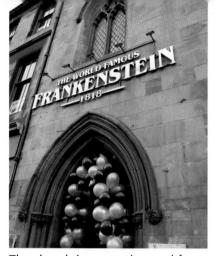

The Augustine United Church on North Bridge is part of the United Reformed Church and is one of the churches in the Synod of Scotland. It was joined in 2005 by members of the former Dalry United Reformed Church.

The church is across the road from the **Frankenstein** pub. Frankenstein's monster gasped its first breath in Mary Shelley's 1818 novel, then came alive before everyone's eyes in a 1931 high-voltage film spectacle, which became the most famous horror film of all time. This is one of the more popular pubs in the city.

The Bedlam Theatre is a venue for the Edinburgh Festival Fringe, situated across the road from the Greyfriar's Bobby statue. The theatre is Scotland's oldest student-run theatre. The Fringe runs in August and showcases new work from around the world. The Royal Mile is full of street entertainers during the Fringe time.

Bristo Square was inaugurated on 5 July 1983 by the principal of the University of Edinburgh. It is now a haven for skateboarders and cyclists.

In this church, dedicated to **St Francis**, the Franciscan Friars ministered to the people of Edinburgh from 1926 to 1988.

George Heriot School was founded as a hospital school in 1628 in imitation of Christ's Hospital in London, and in compliance with the will of George Heriot (1563–1624), a goldsmith and jeweller at the court of King James VI and I. From 1886 it was a day school for boys and since 1979 it has catered for both girls and boys.

The main entrance to the George Heriot School.

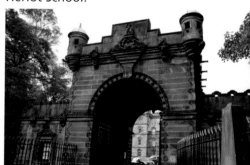

This entrance can be found at the Lloyds TSB building at **East Fountainbridge.**

The back of the **Assembly Halls** can be seen from Princes Street at Mound Place.

At the top of the **Playfair steps** on the Mound is this statue to the memory of officers, non-commissioned officers and men of the Black Watch who fell in the Boer War of 1899–1902.

The Playfair steps pay homage to architect William Henry Playfair (1789–1857). They were opened by the then Lord Provost Kenneth Borthwick on 21 April 1978.

The Mound runs from George IV Bridge down to Princes Street. It was created by the dumping of the earth dug up during the building of the New Town, and around two million cart loads of earth was dumped here in total.

Standing on the Mound you can see the Firth of Forth behind the Scott Monument and Jenners.

The Mound from the New Town and Princes Street leads to the castle and joins the Royal Mile.

The Royal Mile
Introduction

Possibly Edinburgh's oldest street, **the Royal Mile** connects Edinburgh Castle with the Palace of Holyrood House. Visitors will find a lot to explore on either side of this historic road. It earned its regal appellation in the 16th century because it was used by the king to travel between the castle and the palace. It has four sections: Castlehill, Lawnmarket, High Street and Canongate.

Lawnmarket is named after the old linen market which was held here, and it has wider streets than the very narrow Canongate further down. It was once full of dealers and tradesmen who conducted their business in the open rather than in shops.

Canongate was a separate burgh in Edinburgh for over 700 years. It was not named after the cannons from the castle, but canons, or priests, from Holyrood Abbey. As you walk off the High Street down some of the wynds or closes you never know what you will find. Riddle's Court is where the philosopher and historian David Hume once lived. Bailie McMorran also lived here in the late 16th century and entertained James VI and Anne of Denmark here before being killed by pupils of the Royal High School in 1595 during a riot against the reduction in school holidays. Anchor Close was home to a print works which produced the first editions of the *Encyclopaedia Britannica* and Robert Burns's poems. The parents of Sir Walter Scott resided here until 1771.

This close leads to the Jolly Judge's pub, which is located near the Law Courts.

This hidden courtyard contains many carved and inscribed stones, as well as many unusually-arranged sundials.

This emblem, also located near the Law Courts, features a swan and the words 'giving and forgiving'.

The main entrance to the woollen mill has beautiful carvings on the doorway. Situated on the corner of **Cockburn Street**, it offers the very best in textiles and giftware from Scotland.

This old church dating from 1871 is now the **High Street youth hostel**. It offers a cheap, friendly, comfortable and historic place to stay that caters for backpackers, budget travellers, students and world explorers.

This building has these words lit up at night: 'Let us talk about art, maybe.'

There are many tourist and trading shops in Edinburgh with the highest concentration on the Royal Mile. Even as far back as the 1650s a man charged three pence to have a look at a dromedary and a baboon.

This building (pictured top left) used to be the **New Palace Cinema**, beside Fountain Close. Now it is the Scotland shop, selling everything Scottish. Thomas Bassendyne produced the earliest printed copy of the New Testament in Scotland on Fountain Close, and it was also home to the Hall of the Royal College of Physicians, which in turn provided rooms for the publishers Oliver and Boyd from 1778. It is now home to the **Saltire Society**.

You can buy bagpipes here and add to the noise of the city.

This shop is on the main shopping street, Princes Street. Kilts, bagpipes and anything tartan seem to sell the best, just like in the old days of the linen market.

Even **Tintin** cannot resist buying a kilt.

There are many kiltmakers in the city, so Tintin had plenty of choice.

Walking Down the Royal Mile

Just outside the castle esplanade is the Art Nouveau **Witches Well**, marking the spot where more than 300 Edinburgh women were burned at the stake as witches between 1479 and 1722. Jane Douglas was one of them, burned at the stake in 1537. The fountain was designed by John Duncan RSA. The Wicked head and the Serene head signify that some used their exceptional knowledge for evil purposes while others were misunderstood and wished their kind nothing but good. The serpent has the dual significance of evil and wisdom, while the foxglove spray further emphasises the dual purpose of many common objects.

Ramsay Gardens houses some very desirable properties designed by Sir Patrick Geddes in the 19th century. He was a pioneer of architectural conservation and town planning and was known as the 'father of town planning'. These buildings were built around the old Goose Pie House, which was octagonal in shape and was home to the 18th-century poet Allan Ramsay, who wrote *The Gentle Shepherd*.

Looking up at the house you can see many Latin inscriptions, and there is even a dragon below the window ledge.

Cannonball House is home to a stray cannonball which, according to folklore, was fired from the castle during the Rebellion of 1745. However, it is more likely there to mark the high water level of the city's first piped water supply in 1681. It is situated at the top of Castle Wynd.

At **Castle Wynd** there are great views over the city. There are 187 steps in total, and it is a good shortcut for the super fit. A wynd is another name for a close that ran between the lands or tenements.

Across the road from the Witches memorial is **The Witchery** pub. The pub marks the start of The Witchery Tour, which, due to ghostly encounters, visitors take at their own risk. James Boswell (1740–1795) and Dr Samuel Johnson (1709–1784) met and dined in this building in around 1770 according to a plaque on the wall. James Boswell, the Scots writer, was acclaimed for his literary classic *Life of Johnson,* a biography of his illustrious friend Dr Samuel Johnson, the learned scholar, philosopher and critic.

James Boswell and David Hume were residents at **James's Court**, and Boswell's guest Dr Johnson stayed here before going to The Witchery pub for a chat and a light ale. While walking up the High Street the doctor was 'assailed by the evening effluvia of Edinburgh'. *The Builder* journal of 1861 summed up the general atmosphere as follows: 'We devoutly believe that no smell in Europe or Asia can equal in depth and intensity, in concentration and power, the diabolical combination of sulphurated hydrogen, we came upon one evening about ten o'clock in a place called Todrick's Wynd.'

The buildings of the close were destroyed by fire in 1857.

Next to Ramsay Gardens is the **Camera Obscura**, where 'seeing is not believing'. It was set up by an optician called Maria Theresa Short in 1854. Patrick Geddes (1854–1932), who designed Ramsay Gardens, then bought it in 1892. As well as having an exhibition of the history of the camera, a highlight is the giant camera which scans the city and transmits the images live onto a screen for people to watch. There is also a slimatron, where you can lose weight in a matter of seconds, but sadly it is all just an illusion.

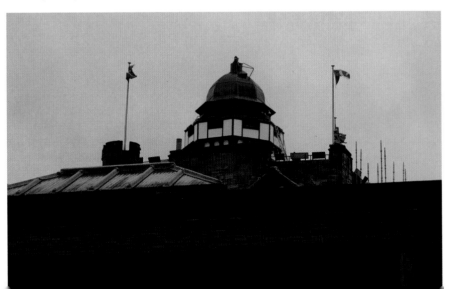

This building used to be Castlehill School for boys and girls, but it is now the **Scottish Whisky Experience**. There is a tour with its own ghost, who shows the visitor the history of whisky.

Tolbooth Kirk has one of the most recognisable spires in the city, designed by Augustus Pugin (1812–1852.) The church was designed by James Gillespie Graham and was originally intended to house the General Assembly of the Church of Scotland, but it was located across the street instead. The building is now called The Hub and has sold tickets for the Edinburgh International Festival since 1999. It has not been a kirk since 1984.

Outside Tolbooth Kirk is a painted cow, **Redburn Dairy,** by Adele Conn. It is cow number 70 and aims to raise money for local charities.

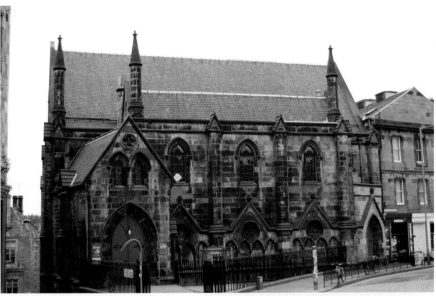

St Columba's by-the-Castle is a Scottish Episcopal church and originally dates back to the 1840s.

An entertainer on the Royal Mile. The guards at the castle can stand at ease.

A plaque on the rear entrance to the **Assembly Halls** states that the Scottish Parliament met here between 1999 and 2004. The Assembly Halls were built in 1859 for the breakaway Free Church, which first met in Tollbooth Kirk.

One of the closes nearest to the castle is **Jollie's Close**.

Mylne's Court was one of the first open squares in Old Edinburgh and was designed by Robert Mylne in the late 17th century. According to a plaque, the old buildings that formed the west side of the court were demolished in 1883. The North and South blocks were restored and the east range rebuilt by the University of Edinburgh between 1966 and 1970. This work was made possible by generous friends of the university.

At **477b Lawnmarket** is Gladstone's Land, an example of 17th-century tenement housing in the Old Town. It has been restored by the National Trust for Scotland. Outside the building there is a gold eagle catching its dinner.

Lady Stair's House is home to the Writers Museum, which celebrates the work of the three great Scottish writers, Robert Burns, Sir Walter Scott and Robert Louis Stevenson.

Lady Stair's Close is where the mansion of Lady Stair was located. It was restored by the 5th Earl of Rosebery, who was a 19th-century Prime Minister.

According to a plaque, Sir Richard Steele gave supper to local beggars in a tavern in 1717.

The first statue you come to while walking down the Royal Mile is in front of St Giles' Cathedral. It is of the philosopher **David Hume** (1711–1776). It was completed in 1995 by Sandy Stoddart, who was determined to build monuments to Scotland's forgotten heroes.

The ornate statue pictured above, decorated with bronze stags, is of the 5th Duke of Buccleuch and 7th Duke of Queensberry, Walter Francis Montagu Douglas Scott, (1806–1884), one of Scotland's richest landowners. He is wearing the Order of the Garter robes and around the statue are various bloody battle scenes. It was unveiled in Parliament Square in February 1888.

The High Kirk of St Giles, officiallly known as the High Kirk of Edinburgh, is the home of Presbyterianism in Scotland. John Knox started the Scottish Reformation from here. He served as minister from 1559 to 1572, preaching his unique message regulating his approach to God in worship. The first St Giles' Kirk was founded in 854.

Inside **St Giles** there is a plaque on the wall to mark where Jenny Geddes launched a protest when Charles I's *Book of Common Prayer* was read out for the first time. A copy of the National Covenant is on display on the wall. The Royalist Marquis of Montrose and the Covenanting Marquis of Argyll, both killed during the Civil War, were executed outside the church and are now entombed within its walls. St Giles was named after the patron saint of cripples and beggars.

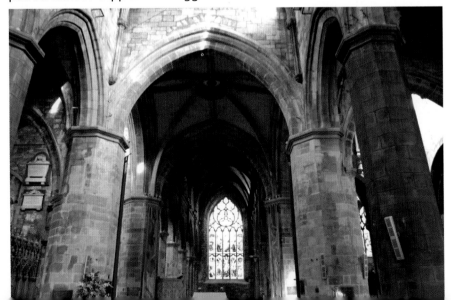

This plaque is in memory of Sir Robert Philip (1857–1939), who was a physician. Near this place, in 1887, he founded a tuberculosis dispensary, the first clinic in the world dedicated to fighting a specific disease. Some 150 years earlier, in 1738, Edinburgh was declared the 'world's leading medical centre'.

Parliament Square is located beside St Giles.

A statue of **King Charles II** on his horse can be found here. He is dressed as a Roman emperor. It was erected in 1685 by James Smith and is one of the oldest lead-cast statues in Britain.

The Tolbooth Prison entrance, demolished in 1817, is marked by the Heart of Midlothian found in the cobblestones. It is traditional to spit on the heart for luck, too late for many prisoners. Sir Walter Scott immortalised the heart in his novel called *The Heart of Midlothian*. It was also the scene for the 1736 Porteous rise. On 14 April 1736 the Scottish poet Allan Ramsay got more than he bargained for when he attended an Edinburgh execution after it turned into the 'Hobleshaw' riot. Hangings in those times were as much a spectator pastime as today's football matches, and a large, somewhat sympathetic crowd had turned out to watch the event. The condemned man, Edinburgh merchant Andrew Wilson, had robbed the customhouse of Pittenweem.

These brass plates mark the site of the old Tollbooth Prison.

Behind St Giles is the replica of the **Mercat Cross** given to the city by the then Prime Minister, Sir William Gladstone. The original Mercat Cross dated from 1365. Proclamations of Parliamentary elections or the ascent of a new monarch to the throne are still made from the cross three days after they are made in London.

Richard Lawson was standing here when he heard trumpets and the Devil telling him who was going to die in battle. He then went on to be the only man named to survive the Battle of Flodden several months later, after praying to God to save his life.

The Law Courts, originally designed by Robert Adam, are where Sir Walter Scott practised law before becoming a writer.

The Signet Library is located on the west side of the square. It is the centre for the Society of Her Majesty's Writers to the Signet, an organisation that originated from the Keepers of the King's Seal. The shell of the library was built in 1810 by Robert Reid, while the interior was designed by William Stark and finished by William Playfair. It contains Parliamentary publications from 1688–1834.

Parliament House was the meeting place of the Scots Parliament between 1639 and 1707.

Pictured above and right is the site of the last public execution in Edinburgh. The site of the gallows is marked by three brass plates at the edge of the pavement in front of the gold plaque. George Bryce, the Ratho murderer, was executed here on 21 June 1864.

Brodie's Close is named after Deacon Brodie, who inspired Robert Louis Stevenson to write a play which then went on to inspire *Dr Jekyll and Mr Hyde*. Brodie was the son of a cabinetmaker in the Lawnmarket. He was hanged near St Giles on 1 October 1788 on a gallows that he himself had designed. By day Brodie was a pious, wealthy and much respected citizen, and in 1781 he was elected Deacon of the city. But at night he was a gambler and thief and his cunning and audacity were unsurpassed.

On the corner of Lawnmarket and Bank Street is the Deacon Brodie pub, named after this villain.

This stone on the pavement quotes Robert Burns. It reads, in a clockwise direction, 'Man to man the world o'er, shall brothers be for a' that.'

Across the road is **Edinburgh City Chambers,** which was designed by John Adam, the brother of Robert Adam. It was built as the Royal Exchange in 1761 before becoming the headquarters of the City Council in the late 19th century. There are many archways leading into the chambers from the Royal Mile.

Advocate's Close was the residence of Lord Advocate Sir James Stewart between 1692 and 1713. It was also the residence of Andrew Crosbie, the jovial Counsellor Pleydell, and Sir John Scougall, who painted William III and Queen Mary.

In the middle of the courtyard is a statue of Alexander and his horse Bucephalus by the well-known sculptor John Steel, casted in 1883.

The old entrance to **Craig's Close**, which closed in 1932 when an extension was built onto the City Chambers. It was named after John Craig, and both Robert Burns and Walter Scott had associations with this close.

Beneath the City Chambers is **Mary King's Close**, which had to be closed off for many years after the plague of 1645. Many a tourist has claimed they have seen a ghost here. The hidden closes include real town houses, streets and rooms dating back to the 1600s. Actors dressed up in period costume try to entice people to look for a ghost themselves.

Hugh Miller (1802–1856) was a geologist and naturalist, writer and folklorist. He edited the *Witness* newspaper at 297 High Street from 15 January 1840 until his death on 24 December 1856. He said 'Life is itself a School, and Nature always a fresh study.'

Fishmarket Close used to be the centre for all things fish-related, and you could smell it from the top of the Royal Mile. It was also home to the City Hangman, the last of whom was John High, who died in the 1820s.

The Lawnmarket Wellhead or cistern was built in 1835. It probably replaced a cistern of 1675, removed when the George IV Bridge was built. The cisterns provided water from Coniston springs for the inhabitants of the Old Town via the Castlehill reservoir, which holds up to 1.5 million gallons. They became important meeting places where long queues used to form. The dents caused by thousands of buckets being placed under the tap can still be seen in the stonework. They fell into disuse in the 19th century when water was supplied to individual houses.

The Old Assembly Close marks the location where dancing assemblies were held in a hall from 1720 to 1766. It also marks the residence of Clement Little, the founder of the University Library, and his brother, Provost William Little.

The Auld Reekies ghost and torture tour begins outside this church on Hunter Square.

There are many ghost tours around Edinburgh, in particular the Old Town around the Royal Mile, which are most effective after the sun has set.

Bailie Fyfe's Close allows you to truly appreciate what life was like centuries ago. It dates back as far as the 1570s. Bailie and Fyfe were magistrates and Gilbert Fyfe lived here between 1677 and 1687.

The Museum of Childhood can be found in Hyndford's Close. It is home to many great toys and playthings of the past. It claims to be 'the noisiest museum in the world'.

131

A memorial above **Paisley's Close** reads 'Heave awa', chaps, I'm no deid yet', which was shouted by a boy as he was dug out of the rubble of the collapsed tenement in 1861. Thirty-five people died in the incident.

This Italian restaurant was formerly the shop of **James Gillespie of Spylaw**, who was a tobacco and snuff manufacturer and the founder of James Gillespie's hospitals and schools. He died on 8 April 1797.

Flora Macdonald attended school near the **Old Stamp Office Close**. She helped Bonnie Prince Charlie sail 'over the sea to Skye' after the Battle of Culloden.

Sir James Simpson, who discovered chloroform, had a medical dispensary on **Carrubber's Close** in the 1860s. The close is thought to be named after William Carriberis, a merchant who lived here in around 1450. In 1736 Allan Ramsay launched a theatre near here, which the magistrates soon closed.

Carrubber's Christian Centre was founded in 1858 as the Carrubber's Close Mission, and is an independent, non-denominational evangelical church. The present building was opened in 1884 and was renovated between 1992 and 1996.

Moubray House dates from the early 16th century. It is believed to be the oldest inhabited house in Edinburgh. In 1706 Daniel Defoe stayed here when he helped negotiate the Act of the Union. A plaque on the wall notes the name George Jamesone, who was a well-known painter in his day, painting for magistrates and royalty. It is next door to John Knox's House.

GOD ·ABVFE· AL ·AND· YI ·NYCHTBOVRGOO

John Knox's House is located at 43–45 High Street. There is no proof that John Knox actually stayed here on the second floor, but it was inhabited by James Mossman, the goldsmith to Mary, Queen of Scots. It is now a museum to the life and work of John Knox.

There are biblical inscriptions on the wall and a sundial can also be seen high above the street.

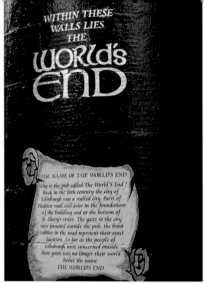

Parts of the Flodden Wall still exist in the foundations of the **World's End** pub and at the bottom of St Mary's Street. The gates to the city were situated outside the pub, and the brass cobbles in the road represent their exact location. As far as the people of Edinburgh were concerned, outside these gates was no longer their world, hence the name World's End.

This funny painting is on the wall outside the World's End pub.

The **SAS Radisson** was built in 1988 using modern methods but in keeping with the traditional looking closes. It is located at the corner of Niddry Street and the Royal Mile. Dickson Close was once a route to The Cowgate.

This **red building** stands out from the rest. A plaque on the wall states that 'Al This Wark was begun be deacon on 10 January 1989 an endit be them on 31 March 1990.'

Looking up above **No.1 High Street** you can see this soldier looking down on you with his sword drawn, just in case you give him any trouble or do not leave after last orders.

The Canongate Christian Institute, dating from 1878.

There are many posters in the windows of people's houses as part of the **Save Our Old Town** (SOOT) campaign. This cartoon has a mother and a child who are speaking to a doorman. The caption reads 'We only went out for a pint of milk, now our home is a 5-star hotel.'

The cross on the roadway marks the site of the original standing **Cross of St John,** which was on the boundary between Edinburgh and the burgh of Canongate. The ancient order of St John is thought to have owned land and property next to the cross during the Middle Ages. The cross was set in place by the Venerable Order of St John of Jerusalem in 1987.

The Knights of St John had their houses in the district around **St John's Pend**.

The entrance to the street was built in around 1768. The houses were occupied by famous families and occasionally by Smollett, according to the plaque on the wall.

Playhouse and **Old Playhouse Close** led to the theatres and hall from 1747 to 1769. Home's *Douglas* was first staged here in 1756.

The Canons' Gait is situated upon the original location of Plainstane's Close, named as such because it was the first close in the Canongate to be paved in the same style as the street. It is thought that in the 16th century this was the residence of Mary, Queen of Scots's French tailor, Jacques de Soulis.

Deacon Brodie's last attempted robbery took place here, at **Chessel's Court**.

These small windows have bars on them for security. A thief would have to be the size of Oliver Twist, not Deacon Brodie, to get in between them.

Morocco Land is a restored early 18th-century tenement and has a figure of a Moor on the wall. It is attached to the story of a local, Andrew Gray, who fled to Morocco after being sentenced to death. He made is fortune and returned to find his cousin had caught the plague. He successfully cured her and they married and lived in Morocco Land.

Tweedale Court is home to a shed (below left) which is thought to have been a sedan chair store. Sedan chairs were used by the gentry in the 18th century.

Tweedale House was built in around 1600. It is a small walk from the main street. In 1750 John and Robert Adam did some work on the building before it became the headquarters of the British Linen Bank. It is now home to the *List* magazine, informing people of events in Glasgow and Edinburgh.

Trinity College Church was founded in around 1460 by Queen Mary of Gueldres, wife of James II. It was intended to move it to a new location in **Chalmers Close** one brick at a time. However, the bricks never made it, being pilfered by the workers, and only the apse was moved.

The Brass Rubbing Centre can now be found here. The centre has an extensive collection of brasses moulded from ancient Pictish stones, rare Scottish brasses and mediaeval church brasses.

On the wall outside Moray House is a plaque in honour of **Sir Godfrey Hilton Thomson** (1881–1935) commissioned by the University of Edinburgh. He was the pioneer of educational testing, Bell Professor of Education and Director of Moray House College.

Moray House was built in 1628 for Mary, Dowager Countess of Home. Her daughter, the Countess of Moray, was given it by her mother. It is believed that Charles I visited here more than once. In 1707 the Treaty of Union was signed here. The current school was created in August 1998 when Moray House Institute of Education merged with the University of Edinburgh, bringing together Moray House, with its origins in the educational developments of the 1830s, and the University's Department of Education, which was the first such department to be established in the Commonwealth.

Canongate Tolbooth, dating from the 16th century, is home to the **People's Story Museum**, which tells the story of the life, work and leisure of ordinary people in Edinburgh from the late 1700s to the present day. The building was used to collect tolls from travellers entering the burgh, but has also served as a council chamber, police court and prison. The prison was tenanted by those who suffered in the cause of liberty, and many of its captives were wrongly detained and brutally treated. A suspected warlock is thought to have been exorcised here, and some Scottish enemies of the state escaped from prison by using strips of blankets and lowering themselves to the ground. The Covenanters were also imprisoned here between 1661 and 1668. Old Tollbooth Wynd is underneath the house.

One of the highlights of **The People's Story Museum** is a reconstruction of an old prison cell.

Tolbooth Tavern is part of the original Canongate Tolbooth, which was built in 1591. This Latin phrase, next to the Tolbooth tavern, *Sic itur ad astra*, translates as 'Thus we do reach the stars.'

Huntly House is the city's official local history **Museum of Edinburgh**, and the building dates from the 16th century. It is named after Duchess Gordon of Huntly, who had a flat here in the 18th century. This museum traces the history of Edinburgh from prehistoric times to the present day.

The Scottish Craft Centre is located next door.

Dunbar Close Garden is a great discovery a few steps from the main street through Dunbar's Close.

The garden is laid out in the character of a 17th-century garden. In 1977 it was donated to the city of Edinburgh by the Mushroom Trust.

There are many benches where you can sit and enjoy your lunch.

On the right-hand side of the garden stands the 18th-century Caddel House and Panmure House, a late 17th-century house where Adam Smith lived from 1778 until his death in 1790. The house was earlier occupied by the Jacobite Earl of Panmure, and Adam Smith was buried just a short walk down the road. It is now only accessible from Little Lochend Close.

There are poppies in the close to mark the fact that it gave access to Lady Haig's poppy factory from 1931 to 1965.

145

Canongate Kirk was built in 1688 to house the expelled congregation from Holyrood Abbey when Scotland was ruled by James II of England.

It states on the wall that 'in 1688 King James VII ordained that the mortification of Thos. Moodie granted in 1649 to build a church should be applied to the erection of this structure'.

This **small monument** in the garden has a unicorn on it, just like the Mercat Cross further up the road at St Giles, and has the dates 1128 and 1888 on the side.

Many great people have been buried in the kirkyard, including **Robert Hurd** (1905–1963), who was an architect and involved in much of the restoration and new building in the Canongate.

You can find his grave by following plaques on the ground.

Adam Smith is buried here. He was the author of *The Wealth of Nations* and lived in Panmure House.

A quote on the tombstone reads 'The Property which every man has in his own labour as it is the original foundation of all other property so it is the most sacred and most inviolable.' Also buried here is Mrs Agnes MacLehose, the Clarinda of Robert Burns's love poems.

David Riccio (1533–66) is believed to be buried here. He was Mary, Queen of Scots's Italian secretary and suspected lover. He was murdered before her eyes in Holyrood Palace, then transported to this graveyard.

This stone, originally erected by Robert Burns, was repaired at the expense of Robert Louis Stevenson, and he re-dedicated it to the memory of Robert Ferguson as the gift of 'one Edinburgh lad to another'.

This tree was planted by **HRH Princess Margaret** on 17 July 1947.

This tree was planted by **HRH Prince Charles** on 22 July 1970.

Robert Ferguson, poet (1750–1774), sculptured by David Annand. Robert Ferguson was born further up the Royal Mile in Cap and Feather Close, which is now demolished. His poetic career lasted only three years, but his work captured the character, spirit, taste and smell of the Edinburgh of his day. One of his best-known poems is called *Auld Reekie*. He even inspired Robert Burns and Robert Louis Stevenson. Robert Burns erected a monument to Ferguson in the graveyard and wrote an epitaph.

Next to the kirk is the **Olde Christmas Shoppe**, also open during the summer months so you can beat the Christmas rush. It has an exclusive range of locally handcrafted festive souvenirs.

This shop is home to the original 'Edinburgh Fudge'. They have been established makers of quality confectionery in the Royal Mile since 1949.

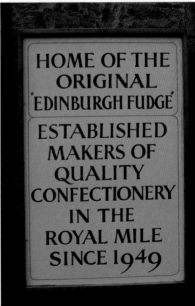

HOME OF THE ORIGINAL "EDINBURGH FUDGE"

ESTABLISHED MAKERS OF QUALITY CONFECTIONERY IN THE ROYAL MILE SINCE 1949

The Canongate Manse.

The Scottish Parliament's **Queensberry House** is located at 64 Royal Mile.

Bakehouse Close is a very beautiful close which leads into the site of the former Scottish and Newcastle Brewery.

Whiteford House occupies the site of the Earl of Winton's town mansion, better known as my Lord Seytoun's lodging in the Canongate.

This is **Milton House Public School**, which has the date 1886 inscribed high above the ground.

There is always time for a game of bowls in Edinburgh.

At the bottom of Canongate is **White Horse Close**. The old stables for Holyrood House were once thought to be here.

The Edinburgh School of English, where you can study English in Scotland.

HOLYROOD

Holyrood Palace was founded as a monastery in 1128. The Palace of Holyroodhouse in Edinburgh is the Queen's official residence in Scotland. Situated at the end of the Royal Mile, the palace is closely associated with Scotland's turbulent past, including Mary, Queen of Scots, who lived here between 1561 and 1567. Successive kings and queens have made the Palace of Holyroodhouse the premier royal residence in Scotland. Today, it is the setting for State ceremonies and official entertaining.

Holyrood Abbey was founded by David I in 1128.

Holyrood Fountain is in the middle of the forecourt. It was made to look like the fountain made for King James V, which is at the Palace of Linlithgow.

On the side of the new **Scottish Parliament building** beside the Canongate there are many plaques built into the wall with sayings and quotes. This plaque quotes from Psalm 19, verse 14.

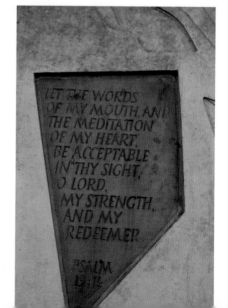

The Wild Boar 2000 by Ronald Rae (born 1946), made from Corrennie granite.

This small building claims to be **Queen Mary's Bath House**, where Mary, Queen of Scots, is thought to have bathed in wine. It was once attached to a boundary wall enclosing the king's privy garden and served as a pavilion or summer house, where the royal family might relax while strolling in the garden.

This inscription on the wall near Holyrood Palace states 'God save the King' with the date 1606. *Beati Pacifici* means 'Blessed are the Peacemakers.'

Scotland's new Parliament sits at the foot of Edinburgh's famous Royal Mile, in front of the spectacular Holyrood Park and Salisbury Crags. Constructed from a mixture of steel, oak and granite, the complex building has been hailed as one of the most innovative designs in Britain today. Drawing inspiration from the surrounding landscape, the flower paintings of Charles Rennie Mackintosh and the upturned boats on the seashore, Enric Miralles, one of the world's premier architects, developed a design that was a building 'growing out of the land'.

The front of the building looks out
on to the Salisbury Crags.

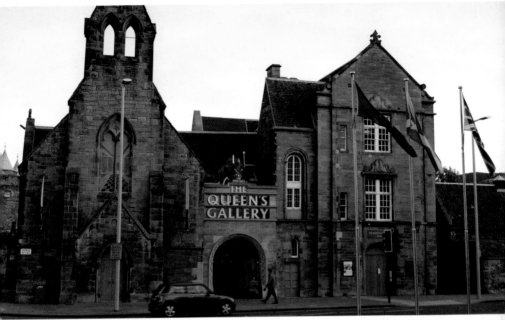

Queen's Gallery at Abbey Strand, set in a former church and school at the entrance to the palace, holds rotating exhibits from the Royal Collection.

If you wanted to be queen for the day, then you could have your pick from these crowns.

Abbey Strand is at the bottom of the Royal Mile and beside Holyrood Palace.

Calton Hill

Calton Hill is one of Edinburgh's main hills, set right in the city centre. It is unmistakable, with its Athenian acropolis poking above the skyline. The acropolis is in fact an unfinished monument, originally called the 'National Monument'. Initiated in 1816, a year after Napoleon's defeat at Waterloo, it w meant to be a replica of the Parthenon in Athens, as a memorial to those who had died in the Napoleonic Wars. Building began in 1822, but funds ran dry, a architect Charles Robert Cockerell never got to see the façade of his building completed. It was dubbed 'Edinburgh's shame' at the time, but it is now a popular landmark and it is a lot of fun crawling up and down its giant steps. Plans to complete the building never really get much support.

Calton Hill is very close to Princes Street and is 350 feet high.

There are great panoramic views over the Firth of Forth...

...and you can also see the Salisbury Crags.

On a clear day you can even see the Forth Road and Rail Bridges.

There is also a great view over the Old and New Towns of Edinburgh...

...and the bridges that link them.

This stone marks the top of Calton Hill. If you want to get an even better view you can climb up on it.

The National Monument, built to remember those Scots who died in the Napoleonic Wars. The money ran out after only 12 columns had been built. Charles Robert Cockerell (1788–1863) was the architect and his young assistant was William Playfair, who went on to design the National Gallery of Scotland and the New Observatory and Dugald Stewart monument, both on Calton Hill.

The Old City Observatory was built by Playfair in 1818 for his uncle, a well-known mathematician and philosopher. When smoke pollution from the trains became too bad at the end of the 19th century it was relocated to Blackford Hill. The Old Observatory is the last surviving building of James Craig, the designer of the New Town.

164

Nelson's Monument stands high up on the hill and above Regent Road. It is 110 feet tall and was built in 1816 to commemorate Nelson's victory at the Battle of Trafalgar.

The monument to **Dugald Stewart,** who lived from 1753 to 1828.

He was not a well-known figure, but was a professor of moral philosophy at Edinburgh University.

It looks like an upturned telescope, which is appropriate as it is beside the observatory. At one o'clock every day a large ball was dropped from the mast at the top to signal the time for ships far out in the Firth of Forth.

This cairn was built by the keepers of the Vigil for a Scottish Parliament. On 11 September 1997 Scotland voted YES YES for her own parliament.

The new Scottish Parliament building can be seen just to the right of this cairn.

Rocks with personal inscriptions make up this monument.

The **Burns Monument** was erected in 1830 to remember Scotland's greatest poet. It was designed by Thomas Hamilton.

St Andrew's House is home to the government offices and was built on the site of Calton gaol. It was built between 1936 and 1939.

The royal coat of arms can be found above the door.

Many figures can also be seen above the main entrance.

The Royal High School dates from 1829 and is modelled on the Temple of Theseus in Athens.

The entrance to **Old Calton burial ground**. It was opened in 1718 for the burial of tradesmen and merchants and was extended in 1767.

Old Calton burial ground contains the **Emancipation Monument** (1893) to the Scottish-American soldiers who died in the American Civil War.

On the top stands **Abraham Lincoln** (12 February 1809 – 15 April 1865), who was the 16th president of the United States, serving from 4 March 1861 until his death on 15 April 1865.

A large memorial to **Thomas Muir**, erected by Thomas Hamilton. It quotes Thomas Muir's speech in the court of the Justiciary on the 10 August 1793. He says 'I have devoted myself to the cause of the people. It is a good cause – it shall ultimately prevail – it shall finally triumph.'

One of the many Celtic crosses, which mark the final resting places of their owners.

This grave is in loving memory of William Wright, who died in 1854.

An arch with the title **Regent's Bridge**, bearing the inscription 'Commenced in the ever memorable year 1815.'

Regent Terrace was designed in 1825 by William Playfair. It sums up the essence of the New Town.

The lights outside the doors are very decorative and are not like the gas lights made famous by the poem called *Leerie* by Robert Louis Stevenson.

The Greenside Hotel, located on Regent Terrace.

Princes Street to Queen Street

One minute you can be looking at clothes on Princes Street, and the next you can be facing the castle.

There is lots to look at above your head as you shop, but try not to walk into other shoppers.

There are no golf courses in the centre of Edinburgh – the nearest is Bruntsfield Links – but at least you can buy your golf clubs cheap at this sale. During the 17th century two English noblemen were challenged by the Duke of York to a game of golf. The two noblemen lost, and the Duke's partner, John Patterson, built a tenement with the money and called it Golfer's Land. It was demolished in 1960. The plaque on the wall had the words 'I hate no person.'

There are no zebra crossings to help you cross this busy street.

Princes Street is the city's main thoroughfare and shopping street.

Jenners is the Harrods of the North and dates from 1837 and claims to be the oldest department store in the world. It was rebuilt in 1892 after a fire. It has a whisky shop with over 400 different varieties, and a toy department to keep the kids amused.

You can have a taste of the Orient for your lunch.

Or if you are celebrating an anniversary you can buy your loved one flowers.

Jenners is located across the road from the Scott Monument.

There are always late-night shoppers here. However, there are no pubs on Princes Street, but plenty of fast food is available.

This bear is opting for the easier way to fish.

Perhaps he would like a deep fried Mars bar to follow.

The **St James's Centre** is not one of the most elegant buildings ever built, but it has many entrances leading into it.

A stone carving states that St James's Square dates from 1779.

A bridge crosses the busy main road.

Another shopping centre is the **Waverley market**, which has a nice open glass design and is a great place to have a coffee and a chat.

The glass roof and entrance allow the light to come in, unlike the dark shopping malls of the 1950s.

The Edinburgh Tourist Centre on Princes Street, with Salisbury Crags and Arthur's Seat in the background.

The home of the new **Family History Centre** used to be the old Register House.

The clock outside the new centre was made by John Ritchie and Son, clockmakers since 1809.

In front of the centre stands *The Iron Duke* in bronze by Steell. The Duke of Wellington sits on his horse as it raises its front legs, getting ready to gallop into battle. It was erected to mark the anniversary of the Battle of Waterloo.

Wellington has great views of the Balmoral Hotel, the Carlton Hotel and the *Scotsman* building.

The Balmoral Hotel is one of Edinburgh's most luxurious hotels and almost makes up for the St James's Centre across the road.

The clock tower on top of the Balmoral Hotel is part of Edinburgh's famous skyline.

Two flags fly above the main entrance.

The Caledonian Hilton is at the other end of Princes Street from the Balmoral, where a doorman welcomes you in.

A man and woman sit above the door just in case the doorman is off duty.

The side of the hotel has many intricate carvings and pillars.

George Street links St Andrew's Square with Charlotte Square and was designed to be the main street of the New Town.

Old and new buildings stand side by side. George Street is said to be haunted by the ghost of Jane Vermelt, who was a corsètiere in George Street.

Even among the bustle of the city streets, it is possible to look down on to the **Firth of Forth**.

This flag is outside the **Norwegian General Consulate**.

A **lighthouse** can be found on the windowledge of this building.

The George Hotel is one of the finest in the New Town.

The Dome Bar and Grill, offering dining and conferencing.

There is a Greek street scene above the main entrance, with children playing and philosophers debating.

Some more of the majestic buildings on George Street.

The Church of St Andrew and St George is famous because it is where the Great Disruption of 1843 took place, when the Church of Scotland was split into two. Some 451 dissenting ministers went on to form the Free Church of Scotland. Today it has an active congregation and seeks to provide a Christian ministry to those who work in the community around it.

New sculptures above the main entrance to the **Capitol building** on George Street.

Lakeland's shop on the corner of George Street and Hanover Street. *Anchora salutis* translates as the 'Anchor of salvation.'

Always cross at the zebra crossing; there are no pelican crossings on this road.

The **Melville Monument** in the centre of St Andrew Square is of Henry Dundas, first Viscount Melville (1742–1811), who was a statesman, a lawyer and the 'uncrowned King of Scotland'. It was modelled by Francis Chantrey and Robert Forrest and is 41 metres high. The statue of Dundas was placed on top of the imposing Roman style column in 1828, and he has dominated the St Andrew Square skyline ever since. The garden is currently undergoing a makeover. The foundation stone for the monument was laid on 18 April 1821.

St Andrew Square was once a most fashionable place to live. Harvey Nichols is a great addition to the square. It was built on the site of the old St Andrew bus station.

When you look up there are many statues on this building at the corner of **West Register Street**.

The statue outside the Royal Bank of Scotland headquarters is of **John, Fourth Earl of Hopetoun**. It was erected with the gratitude of his countrymen.

The headquarters of the **Royal Bank of Scotland** stands out from the rest of the square. The building dates back to 1772 and belonged to Sir Laurence Dundas. It was built by William Chambers and incorporated by Royal Charter in 1727. The domed ceiling was added in the 1850s.

Charlotte Square was designed by Robert Adam in 1791. Many bankers, accountants and lawyers work here.

Bute House, at No. 6, is the official residence of the Secretary of State for Scotland. The Moderator of the General Assembly of the Church of Scotland lives on the upper floor of No. 7.

The lower floors of No. 7 make up the **Georgian House**, which allows visitors to see what it was like to live there in the early 19th century. The first owner was John Lamont of Lamont, at the end of the 18th century. He was the 18th chief of Clan Lamont.

Lord Lister lived here at Charlotte Square between 1870 and 1877.

West Register House was originally St George's Church. It was first designed by Robert Adam, but he died in 1792 and his plans never made it off the ground. The building was built by Robert Reid in 1811. St George's was originally built in 1784 to a design by Major Andrew Frazer. When St George's Church became West Register House in Charlotte Square, the two congregations united to form this congregation in 1964.

In the middle of the square is a statue of **Prince Albert** mounted in Field Marshal's uniform. It was erected by John Steell, who went on to be knighted.

The grass area in the centre is private grounds.

This makes an ideal spot to practise your fishing techniques.

New Town Highlights

The Scottish National Portrait Gallery is dedicated to the illustration of Scottish history, according to an edifice on the wall gifted by John Ritchie Findlay in 1890.

Looking up, there are many beautiful designs and carvings on the wall, including the Glasgow coat of arms.

Almost half the city was reported to have attended the funeral of **Thomas Chalmers**, the leader of the Free Church of Scotland in the 1840s, whose statue faces the castle.

In the middle of Hanover Street is a statue of **George IV** in a kilt by Sir Francis Chantrey commemorating his visit to Edinburgh in 1822. It was the first visit by a reigning monarch for almost 200 years.

The **Lloyds TSB** bank on Hanover Street.

These interesting **warriors** can be seen outside Starbucks off George Street. J.K. Rowling wrote her *Harry Potter* novels in coffee shops in Edinburgh.

A **modern health club** in an old building on Queen Street, but with all the hills and wynds around Edinburgh, it is easy to keep fit.

The entrance to the **British Linen Bank** is very grand.

Rose Street has many pubs, and people taking part in pub crawls, especially during the Rugby World Cup in 2007.

There is a rose decoration in the ground very similar in design to the Heart of Midlothian on the Royal Mile.

New Register House was one of the best buildings designed by Robert Adam; built between 1774 and 1827 to house Scotland's legal and historical public records. It was opened in 1861 and is the headquarters of the Scottish Record Office. Documents dating back to the early 13th century are stored here.

The **Guildford Arms** pub, next door to the New Register House at the start of Rose Street.

St Stephen's Church was designed in 1829 by William Henry Playfair. Its clock claims to have the longest pendulum in Europe at an amazing 65ft 9in. A plaque above the door mentions the Right Honourable William Trotter of Ballindean, Lord Provost of the City.

A smaller Episcopal Church across the road from St Stephen's is **St Vincent's Church**.

There is a small light outside St Vincent's Church.

At this end of the city there are new houses being built, the 'New' New Town.

This **old synagogue** has been transformed into a casino, just beside Princes Street at Shandwick Place.

St Mary's Episcopalian Cathedral was designed by Gilbert Scott in his traditional Gothic style. The Western Towers are called Mary and Barbara after two sisters who left a fortune towards the building of the cathedral. It was completed in 1917 and is Scotland's second-largest church.

The William Gladstone Memorial was created by JP MacGillvray in 1902 to celebrate William Ewart Gladstone (1809–1898), who was several times Prime Minister and MP for Midlothian.

Around the cathedral are houses, and at the end of the street there is usually a corner shop or post office.

This **Tudor house** is a bit out of place beside St George's West Church centre.

In and Around
Princes Street Gardens

If you wanted to sit and have a coffee outside, **Princes Street Gardens** would be the ideal choice. They were formed by the draining of the Nor' Loch in the late 1760s.

During all the hot sunny days in Edinburgh, you can always cool off with a nice ice cream and sit in the park. For the other 360 days you can sit in the rain enjoying your ice cream.

If you want something hot to drink to warm you up there are many cafés and tearooms around Prince Street Gardens. The first coffee house was founded in the city in 1678.

There are great views of the National Gallery and the castle to enjoy while reading your paper or book.

The gardens close at night.

The Scott Monument is over 200 feet high and was built in 1844 as a tribute to Sir Walter Scott by George Kemp.

Sir Walter Scott sits with his favourite deerhound Maida beside him. His memorial was carved from a single 30 tonne block of white Italian marble.

Around the monument are 64 characters from Sir Walter Scott's novels. The monument is open throughout the year.

If you can climb the 290-step staircase, the reward is breathtaking views over the city.

There are many war memorials around the gardens, for example this **War Memorial Boulder**. During the war years of 1940 and 1945 the Norwegian Brigade and other army units were raised and trained in Scotland. Here they found hospitality, friendship and hope during dark years of exile. This memorial is in grateful memory of their friends and allies on these isles. The stone was erected in 1978.

This Norway Maple and the golden Leyland cypress trees were presented by the **Royal Scots (the Royal Regiment)** in 1983 to commemorate the 350th anniversary of the raising of the regiment.

This stone was erected on 14 May 1995 to commemorate the 50th anniversary of the **Liberation of Belsen Concentration Camp** by the British army. It stands in memory of the six million Jews and other innocent victims of Nazi atrocities during World War Two, and those who came together in the united forces to liberate Europe from fascism. 'May their sufferings not have been in vain.'

This tree was planted on 8 February 2001 by the children of the Edinburgh Hebrew congregation in memory of **Anne Frank**, who died in Bergen-Belsen in March 1945, aged 15 years.

This tree was planted by the children of the Edinburgh Hebrew congregation on 27 January 2001 (the first national Holocaust Memorial Day) in memory of those innocent victims who perished in the Holocaust.

A large semi-circular **War Memorial** in Princes Street Gardens.

Waverley Station was built where the church used to be. In 1842 the railway line was open to the public and the station, covering 70,000 square metres, was completed in 1902.

This **large rock** outside Princes Street Gardens, across the road from Waverley Station, was presented in 1966 by Lyndsay D. Gumley II.

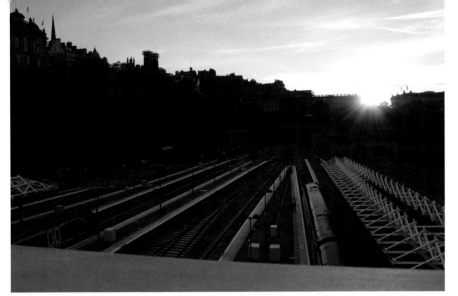

There is a train to Glasgow every 15 minutes during the day. In 1749 the first stagecoach service was started between Glasgow and Edinburgh. It was not until 1765 that these coaches started to run daily, and by 1819 there were five coaches a day.

There are also statues of famous people to be found around the Princes Street Gardens. **Adam Black** (1784–1874) was Provost of Edinburgh, Member of Parliament and founder, in 1807, of the publishing house of A&C Black.

John Wilson was born on 18 May 1785 and died on 1 April 1854.

David Livingston was a
missionary and explorer of Africa.

Sir James Simpson (1811–1870)
discovered chloroform as an
anaesthetic.

Dr Thomas Guthrie DD
(1803–1873) wanted to educate
those living in the slums; he was a
preacher and a philanthropist.

Allan Ramsay (1686–1758) was a
great Scottish poet.

Allan Ramsay frequented **Jenny Ha's Tavern** on the Royal Mile. Luckily for him the old law of 1699 forbidding employment of women in taverns had been challenged and severed.

The Ross Open Air Theatre is used for many events and is the focus for many Hogmanay revellers.

The **Robert Viscount Melville** statue looks onto Princes Street and the castle. He was born on 14 March 1771 and died on 10 June 1851. It was erected to commemorate the regard and esteem of friends and fellow countrymen.

The Ross Fountain was made of eastern iron at the foundry of Antonine Durenne near Paris, France, and was shown at the exhibition of 1862 in London. Daniel Ross, a local gunmaker interested in art and natural science, bought and gifted the fountain to the city of Edinburgh. It was shipped in 122 pieces and arrived in Leith in September 1869. Sadly, he died before the fountain was operational in 1872. The figures were sculpted by Jean-Baptiste Klagmann, who also made works for the Louvre and de Medei fountains in Paris. The first tier has lion's head spouts and mermaid figures with flowing urns, sitting on scallop-shell basins. The four upper figures depict science, art, poetry and industry. At the top a beautifully-modelled figure holds a cornucopia, a cup of plenty. In 2001 the fountain was fully restored in a collaboration between the City of Edinburgh and East of Scotland Water.

Just outside the gardens are the **National Gallery of Scotland and Royal Scottish Academy**. The National Gallery of Scotland was also built by William Playfair. Both have grand pillars and look like Greek temples.

It is now more common to look at the flowers than at how to storm the castle.

The **Royal Scottish Academy,** the Scott Monument and the Balmoral Hotel.

The Royal Scottish Academy looks majestic at sunset.

A large sphinx sits on top of the pillars.

This housed an exhibition of Andy Warhol's work, including his most recognisable piece of work, the Campbell's soup can.

The back of the **Royal Scottish Academy** from the top of the Playfair steps.

This relief was crafted to enable people with impaired vision to enjoy the grandeur of the city. It was presented to the City of Edinburgh by the staff of Marks and Spencer, Edinburgh, in 1984 to mark the company's centenary.

There are also two churches near the gardens, **St John's** and **St Cuthbert's**. The St John the Evangelist Church was designed by William Burn in 1818.

This sculpture outside St John's is called *Famine*, completed in 1985, set in granite and sculpted by Ronald Rae FRBS.

Another neighbouring sculpture is called *Mark of the Nail* and was created in 1985.

The graveyard of St John's has many tombstones of various sizes and details.

This view of the castle is from outside St Cuthbert's Church.

Next door to St John's is **St Cuthbert's Church and graveyard**. It is located on the oldest church site in the city, dating back to the reign of Malcolm III. The church was designed at the turn of 19th century by architect and photographer Hippolyte J. Blanc.

St Cuthbert's viewed from the Ross Fountain inside Princes Street Gardens.

The interior of St Cuthbert's is very beautiful.

Inside the church, near this spot, John Napier is buried, who died on 4 April 1617 aged 67.

Thomas de Quincey is buried outside. He wrote *Confessions of an English Opium Eater*.

The Watchtower outside St Cuthbert's is a reminder of the Burke and Hare days when graves had to be guarded against robbers. Burke and Hare robbed graves of bodies required for medical research. Burke was sentenced to death for murder in 1829 and his trial started on 24 December 1828.

George Kemp, builder of the Scott Monument, is buried in St Cuthbert's graveyard.

The graveyard is cut in two by the railway line.

Finally, if you want to sit and look at the shoppers or catch your breath, then why not take a seat on one of the many benches? This bench was presented by the Boy Scouts Association of the City of Edinburgh and Leith to commemorate the centenary of the birth of the founder, Lord Baden-Powell of Gilwell, and the Jubilee of scouting.

This bench on Princes Street is in loving memory of Mr and Mrs A.W. Cave.

South of the City

The Tollcross Clock, which was once located at the exact geographical centre of the city.

St Mary's Catholic Cathedral is found near the Tollcross Clock.

From Tollcross, it is possible to see the castle high up on the hill.

This foot sculpture is placed outside the cathedral.

The glasshouse next door to a new shopping mall.

The Playhouse stages musicals including *South Pacific*. It is Scotland's 'national' theatre.

Broughton St Mary's Parish Church.

This sculpture is called **Dreaming Spires** and was created in 2005 by Helen Denerley. There is also a poem beside it by Roy Campbell dating from 1946.

Mansfield Place Church dates from the late 19th century and is now the Phoebe Traquair Centre. She was a famous muralist.

If you want some peace and quiet then there is a large grass area called **The Meadows**. The Meadows used to be the former Burgh Muir before it was drained in the 18th century.

There is a children's playpark with swings, roundabouts and slides.

You can play croquet at the **Meadows Croquet Club**, play golf or simply have a picnic and read.

This monument is for the Right Honourable Thomas Clark, Lord Provost of the city.

St Michael and All Saints Church is a Category A-listed Victorian Gothic building and was designed by Sir R. Rowand Anderson (who also designed the Scottish National Portrait Gallery and the McEwan Hall).

There is a crucifix on the side wall of the church.

Sir Robert Rowand Anderson designed the **University of Edinburgh's Graduation Hall** in 1874. The inside imitates a Greek theatre with two tiers of galleries and a half-domed ceiling, with painted figures representing the Arts and Sciences by William Paulin.

The University Union, which dates back to 1889.

There are more **Lion and Unicorns** at the university.

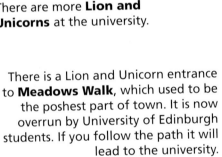

There is a Lion and Unicorn entrance to **Meadows Walk**, which used to be the poshest part of town. It is now overrun by University of Edinburgh students. If you follow the path it will lead to the university.

Edinburgh International Conference Centre was designed by Terry Farell and built in 1995.

The **Point building** at East Fountainbridge.

Police on horses patrol the streets; they are sometimes faster than the cars.

Clydesdale Bank plaza at 50 Lothian Road.

The **New Odeon** cinema building.

The new Standard Life building, which is very different from…

…**the old Standard Life building,** which has more detail in its architecture.

A bridge links Clydesdale Bank
Plaza and the Standard Life
Building.

The **Usher Hall** on Lothian Road is a landmark in the heart of the city and
for the best part of a century it has hosted some of the greatest concerts
and events. The building of the concert hall was funded by Andrew Usher,
a whisky distiller.

There are many decorations and carvings on display high up on the walls.

The **Shakespeares** pub on Lothian Road is right next door to the Usher Hall.

The **Traverse Theatre** is located next to the Usher Hall, having moved from the Royal Mile.

The **Bell Tower** outside the Usher Hall was presented to the City of Edinburgh by Arthur Bell and Sons Ltd, Scotch whisky distillers in Perth in 1962.

The **Sheraton** is situated in the shadow of Edinburgh Castle and is just a short walk from the city's famous shopping thoroughfare, Princes Street.

It is the perfect spot from which to explore the history of the mediaeval Old Town and the architectural interest of the Georgian New Town.

This statue outside the Sheraton Grand is called ***Woman and Child***. It was erected by the City of Edinburgh District Council to honour all those killed or imprisoned for their stand against apartheid. It was unveiled on 22 July 1986 by Suganya Chetty and was sculpted by Ann Davidson. 'Victory is certain.'

The **Filmhouse** is Edinburgh's publicly-funded 'arthouse' cinema and is a hub for the city's film buffs. It has the most varied programme of alternative film, ranging from arthouse and foreign cinema to mainstream second-run films. It is also the location of the Central Box Office for the annual Edinburgh Film Festival, with other off-beat festivals thrown in throughout the year. The Edinburgh Film Guild was established in 1929, being the founders of the Edinburgh International Film Festival and the Filmhouse.

The **Royal Lyceum Theatre** is a beautiful Victorian building with a long history. Built in 1883, its early days saw performances by the likes of Henry Irving and Ellen Terry, while being run by legendary theatre managers Howard and Wyndham. Throughout the 20th century and into the 21st, the building has remained a theatre space and was taken over in 1965 by the Royal Lyceum Theatre Company.

The **Bank of Scotland New Uberior House** offices.

The **Central Hall** at 2 West Tollcross is over 100 years old. The wonderfully-decorative Art Nouveau-style interior is complete with mosaics and stained glass.

The **King's Arms** pub displays the royal coat of arms, with the lion sticking out his tongue, above the door.

The **King's Theatre**, Edinburgh, was built in 1905 by local builder William Stewart Cruikshank. Andrew Carnegie laid the foundation stone and the theatre was opened in 1906 with a performance of *Cinderella* and was managed by A. Stewart Cruikshank. The King's Theatre became the headquarters of Howard and Wyndham and they held their board meetings there. Famously, their AGM on Christmas Eve guaranteed minimal interference from shareholders!

The **Auld Toll** pub and the Barclay Church of Scotland.

The **Barclay Church of Scotland** was designed by Pilkington. It was opened for worship in 1864. Barclay is a diverse congregation – from families who have worshipped in the church for many years to young professional workers, students and international students who become part of the congregation while staying in Edinburgh.

Two angels stand guard above
one of the entrances.

This angel can be found on the
side of the building.

Chambers Street, in the south of the Old Town, was named after William Chambers of Glenormiston, the Lord Provost of Edinburgh. He was the main proponent of the 1867 Edinburgh Improvement Act, which allowed permission for the street's construction.

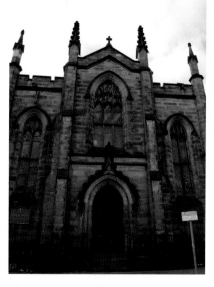

Jericho House, a residential care home for men and women.

The **Museum of Scotland** is located next door to the **Royal Museum** and was opened in 1998. It was designed by Benson and Forsyth and adds a modern feel to the city. The museum tells the story of Scotland and her people.

The Royal Museum is part of the National Museums of Scotland and contains artefacts from around the world, including geology, archaeology, natural history, science, technology and art. Dolly, the first cloned sheep, can be found here.

Queen Victoria's head can be seen above the road.

William Chambers of Glenormiston LLD, Lord Provost of Edinburgh (1865–1869), who was born on 16 April 1800 and died on 21 May 1883, looks on to the Royal Museum.

The **Crown Office** at 25 Chambers Street…

…and the **Sheriff Court** is next door at 27 Chambers Street. They were built recently, in the 1990s.

The old **Edinburgh Dental Hospital and School**, now a pub selling vodka and food.

Grassmarket

The **Grassmarket** is a great place for a drink. Robert Burns stayed in the White Hart Inn during his last visit to Edinburgh in 1791. In 1803 Dorothy Wordsworth also stayed here.

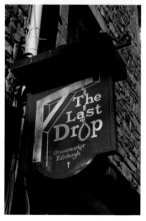

This pub has an unfortunate name, **The Last Drop**, but it is a reference to the hangings that took place near by.

It is possible to walk up to the castle from the Grassmarket, but not after visiting all the pubs.

There are **public clothes poles** in the Grassmarket.

There are great views of the castle from outside the pubs.

The **Scottish flag** flies high above one of the pubs.

The **Memorial Garden** at the top of the Grassmarket was opened by His Grace Douglas, 14th Duke of Hamilton, in the presence of the Lord Provost, magistrates and council of the City of Edinburgh and a large public assembly on 24 October 1954. Many martyrs and Covenanters died for the Protestant faith on this spot.

An organised sign telling you where to go, but not to be read after some light ales

This is the **New Greyfriar's Mission Building**, to the glory of God and in loving memory of the Revd William Robertson DD for nearly 40 years minister at this parish.

The **West Bow Well** was erected by the town council in 1674.

The Latin phrase *Nisi Dominus Frustri* has been associated with Edinburgh since 1647. It translates as 'Except the Lord in vain' and is taken from Psalm 127.

Victoria Street is a very steep, cobbled street with many different shops catering for many different tastes. There are many novelty and joke shops located here.

Dean Village

The Leith walkway passes under Dean Bridge. This little river flows from the Pentland Hills to the Port of Leith, where it enters the Firth of Forth. The Port dates from 1330.

Dean Village was a philanthropic housing scheme for the local mill workers. It has a unique character all its own and is proud of its sense of community. The villagers have recently united to form the Dean Village Association, dedicated to the physical and social conservation of this beautiful and tranquil part of Edinburgh.

Dean Bridge was built in 1832 by Thomas Telford. It is 100 feet high.

St Bernard's Mineral Well can be found on the walkway.

The Doric temple on top was built by Alexander Naysmith in 1789.

The well was restored in 1888 and a sculpture by David Stevenson called *Hygeia* was placed inside. The mineral spring had long been thought to offer health-giving properties.

Next to the well is a memorial to William Nelson. Words along the top read 'The Liberal Deviseth Liberal things.'

A plaque near Dean Bridge has a quotation from the Bible, Genesis chapter 3, verse 19. It reads 'In the sweat of thy face, shall thou eat bread.'

The **French consulate generale** at 11 Randolph Crescent.

The earliest mills at **West Mill** are recorded from 1463 and were owned by the town council of Edinburgh. This building was erected in 1805 by the Guild of Bakers, whose emblem was a wheatsheaf.

This millstone, originally from France, marks the site of **Lindsay's Mill**, one of 11 water-powered mills that worked here in the 17th century. The weir held back enough water to drive the mills.

The Water of Leith Walkway is 12 miles long, from Balerno to Leith.

Leith

The Firth of Forth provided abundant fish for the earliest inhabitants who developed the village around the river mouth. The earliest cottages in what came to be known as Leith were built where the river met the Forth Estuary. The first records were scanty, written by monks as early as 1143. Leith developed into the major port of Scotland until it was overtaken by the Clyde. It led to the dereliction of warehouses and gap sites proliferated. In the last 20 years the 'gentrification' of Leith has proved extremely successful, encouraging more small businesses to set up in the area. Restaurants and bars around areas such as The Shore will also continue to take advantage of the development of converted warehouses and the attractive waterfront. The former royal residence of the Queen and family at sea, the Royal Yacht *Britannia*, is a major tourist attraction.

You can see the **Forth Road and Rail Bridges** from Leith. On 4 March 1890 the last rivet was driven into the bridge and it was declared open. By the time the painters have finished painting the bridge, they have to start it again.

The Forth Bridges consist of a road bridge (left) and a rail bridge (right).

There are many new developments around Leith.

An **old cannon**, which is tiny compared to Mon's Meg at Edinburgh Castle.

The Shore was the original port of Leith and Edinburgh.

Tall-masted sailing ships berthed here, while scores of crewmen loaded fish, coal and grain. This site is now the **Ocean Terminal and Leisure Complex**.

This bust is of the Governor of New South Wales (1795–1800), **John Hunter**, who was born in Leith in 1737.

Many buildings remind the visitor of the harbour's early past.

The **Victoria Swing Bridge** was completed in 1874, carrying double rail and road tracks with a footpath along each side. When it was built it was the largest swing bridge in the United Kingdom.

The **Malmaison Hotel** was built in the Scottish Baronial style and opened in 1885 as the Sailors' Home. Now it caters for a different category of clientele and provides more luxurious standards of accommodation.

Leith has always had a large trade with **Hamburg and Rotterdam**.

On The Shore the harpoon is a reminder of whaling, which in its day was a valuable source of food, oils and raw materials for industry. Whaling ceased as late as 1963.

Britannia is now located at the Ocean terminal shopping centre in Leith, just two miles from the city centre. *Britannia*, with its luxurious five decks, was the perfect royal residence for the Queen and royal family.

The **Docks at Leith** are still operational, with military ships docked alongside the Royal Yacht *Britannia*.

As you walk up from Leith into the city you pass the **Corn Exchange**, completed in 1862 at a cost of £6,500.

The **Midlothian County Buildings**, home of the registrar's office.

The **Leith Assembly Rooms** incorporated the original Assembly Hall of 1783 on Assembly Street in 1809. There is a plaque on the wall which was unveiled by the Rt Hon. Norman Irons, Lord Provost of Edinburgh, on 31 October 1994, the 250th anniversary of the birth of James Craig (1744–1795), who was the planner of Edinburgh's first New Town and the architect of this building.

South Leith Parish Church was built in 1483 by the trade guilds of Leith and dedicated to St Mary, patron saint of sailors.

A statue of **Robert Burns** was erected by the Leith Burns Appreciation Society in 1898. A plaque on one side was presented by William Tulloch. It quotes 'in order, on the hearth-stane, the luggies three are arranged' from *Halloween*.

A statue of Queen Victoria (1837–1901), the Empress of India from 1877 to 1901. It was erected in 1907 and was unveiled with great pomp and ceremony. In 1913 two side panels were added to commemorate Queen Victoria's visit to Leith in 1843 and her review of volunteers who were to serve in the Boer War. She did not actually land in Leith but passed through on her way to visit the Duke of Buccleuch.

The Outskirts

Fettes College was built with a trust of over half a million pounds from the estate of Sir William Fettes, who died in 1836. Many well-known politicians studied here, the most famous being the previous Prime Minister Tony Blair.

James Bond was supposed to have gone to school here after he was expelled from Eton, and it is claimed that Sean Connery delivered milk here in the 1950s. Fettes can be seen from many streets away.

Above right: Outside is this **commemorative stone**, which was laid by W.H. Lely on 3 October 1964 to mark the centenary of Fettes College.

Outside the main grounds can be found this very prestigious set of gates.

A war memorial to the glorious memory of Fettiesians who gave their lives for their country in the war of 1914–18. A kilted soldier raises his arm, while written in stone underneath are two words: 'Carry On.'

Haymarket Station used to be the headquarters for the Edinburgh and Glasgow Railway.

This **clock tower** across the road from Haymarket train station is in honoured memory of the players and members of the Heart of Midlothian football club who lost their lives in World War Two, 1939–45.

Daniel Stewart's and Melville College is a very grand Victorian building in Jacobean style. It is a private school with over 700 pupils. Its motto is 'Never Unprepared', which is the same as the Clan Johnston.

The college has many turrets and towers.

William Playfair designed **Donaldson's School** in 1841. It was damaged by a bomb dropped from a Zeppelin in 1916.

The **National Gallery of Modern Art** is home to Scotland's outstanding national collection of modern and contemporary art. The gallery is set in extensive parkland, where visitors can discover sculpture works by important artists like Ian Hamilton Finlay, Henry Moore, Rachel Whiteread and Barbara Hepworth. The Gallery of Modern Art shows special exhibitions and works from around 1900 to the present day.

This double standing pin is simply called **Untitled** and is by Gerald Laing, born in 1936.

Landform, created by Charles Jencks in 2002, can be seen as you drive into the grounds on the left. This dramatic work comprises a stepped, serpentine mound reflected in three crescent-shaped pools of water.

The **Royal Botanic Gardens** is located north of the city in Inverleith district. It moved here in 1820–23 and the west entrance is currently undergoing redevelopment. It is located within 72 acres of beautiful trees and plants from all over the world and is a scientific research institution with a worldwide reputation for the study of plants and their diversity.

The **Queen Mother's Memorial Garden** was opened by Her Majesty the Queen on Friday 7 July 2006.

The **Victorian Palm House**.

Murrayfield Stadium, home of the Scottish national rugby team. The very first rugby international match was played at Raeburn Place, Edinburgh, on Monday 27 March 1871, on the cricket field of the Edinburgh Academy. Murrayfield was officially opened on a sunny day on 21 March 1925. England were the visitors and a more fitting climax to the international season could not have been scripted: it was pure *Boy's Own* stuff!

This **archway** outside Murrayfield is in proud memory of the Scottish rugby players who gave their lives in the World Wars. The archway, which had been erected at Inverleith in 1921, was transferred to Murrayfield in 1936.

In 1929 the **Clock Tower** was gifted by Sir David McGowan, a past president of the union. Still a landmark today, although having been removed from its previous location at the top of the terracing at the Railway End when the stadium underwent major renovation and rebuilding in the early 1990s, the clock tower is now located at the rear of the East Stand. In 1930 J. Aikman Smith, a past president and former secretary and treasurer of the union, presented the first score box, and in 1931 Sheriff Watt KC presented the original flagstaff and flag.

Edinburgh Zoo is the largest in Scotland. It is set on steep hills and consists of around 80 acres of land. The penguins are a must see, with their daily march at 2pm. In just one day you can meet over 1,000 wonderful animals in beautiful parkland on the outskirts of Edinburgh, and you can also enjoy a wide range of visitor facilities, from free Hilltop Safari rides to the top of the hill, to children's play areas, restaurants, gift shops and masses of events and activities throughout the year.

The **king penguin** is the largest of the penguin species kept at Edinburgh Zoo. At an average height of 90cm, it towers above the gentoos and the crested rockhoppers. It is the second-largest species of penguin in the world, only smaller than the emperor penguin. The small self-sustaining colony of penguins dates back to 1910. The kings were among the earliest animals in the zoo and were originally wild.

The **grevy's zebra** is one of three zebra species, although these three species are only distantly related. The mountain and common zebras are physically similar, as they both resemble striped horses with only slight differences in size and stripe pattern. However, the Grevy's zebra is quite different to its two relatives.

This **polar bear** is called Mercedes, and her ancestors only recently evolved from the brown bear, as the last Ice Age took effect. It is the largest of the seven species of bear, feeding on seal pups, fish and, in summer, berries. An interesting fact about polar bears is that their skin is black.